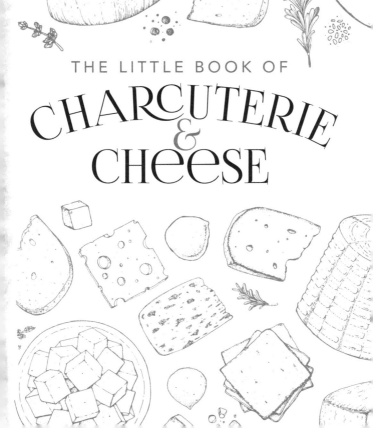

THE LITTLE BOOK OF

CHARCUTERIE
&
Cheese

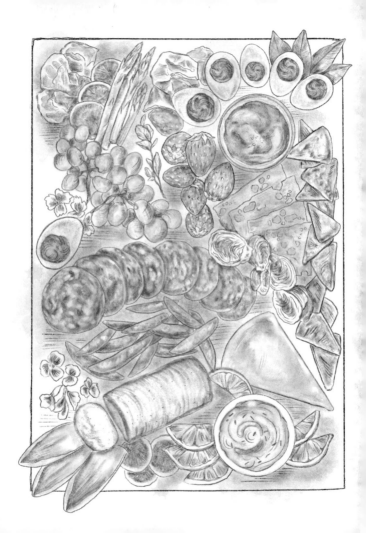

INTRODUCTION

Entertaining couldn't be simpler and more fun than with a charcuterie and cheese board. We eat with our eyes and, yes, our fingers too. A charcuterie and cheese board checks both boxes with flying colors. Decorative boards are bountiful and beautiful. From simple and rustic to abundant and lavish, there's a board for every season, group size, and event.

Food on boards makes entertaining a breeze; they can be arranged in advance and adapted to suit diets and tastes. Most important, charcuterie and cheese boards are relaxed and social, the epitome of finger food, presented family–style and inviting grazing and interaction.

HOW CAN
YOU GOVERN
A COUNTRY
WHICH HAS 246
VARIETIES OF
CHEESE?

—CHARLES DE GAULLE

contents

MY WIFE AND I LOVE TO
HOST WINE AND CHEESE
PARTIES. THEY ARE SIMPLE
AND ELEGANT AND
YOU DON'T HAVE TO
PUT A LOT OF EFFORT
AND TIME INTO IT.

—Tyler Florence

THE LITTLE BOOK OF

CHARCUTERIE
&
CHEESE

LYNDA BALSLEV

Andrews McMeel
PUBLISHING®

Andrews McMeel Publishing
a division of Andrews McMeel Universal
1130 Walnut Street, Kansas City, Missouri 64106
www.andrewsmcmeel.com

23 24 25 26 27 SHO 10 9 8 7 6 5 4 3 2 1

ISBN: 978-1-5248-7804-7

Library of Congress Control Number: 2022949708

Illustrations on pages ii, 32, 36, 40, 46, 68, 86,
98, 112, 120, and 124 by Parmeet Birdi

All other illustrations © Getty Images

Editor: Jean Lucas
Art Director/Designer: Diane Marsh
Production Editor: Meg Utz
Production Manager: Chadd Keim

ATTENTION: SCHOOLS AND BUSINESSES
Andrews McMeel books are available at quantity
discounts with bulk purchase for educational, business,
or sales promotional use. For information, please
e-mail the Andrews McMeel Publishing Special
Sales Department: sales@amuniversal.com.

CHARCUTERIE HISTORY & TYPES

While charcuterie and cheese are the board stars we enjoy today, their roots are intertwined in history with practical origins.

CHARCUTERIE

CHARCUTERIE IS A FRENCH TERM
(CHAIR=FLESH + CUIT=COOKED)
THAT REFERS TO THE TRADITION OF
PREPARING AND PRESERVING MEATS.

The Italian term is salumi. Historically, these methods were essential to preserve meat without refrigeration. Salting, dry-curing, and smoking meats are ancient methods that produce sausage and salami, pâtés and confit, as well as dried, cured, and smoked meats. Today, the term "charcuterie" has evolved to reflect the art of assembling an assortment of cured meats and cheese, as well as breads, pickles, and other artisan products and accompaniments.

SALAMI is ground meat mixed with fat, wine, and spice, then stuffed in casings and dried. Common types are Spanish chorizo, French sauçisson sec, Italian soppressata, Calabrese, and Genoa salami. To serve salami, thinly slice and layer or fan on a board. If the slices still have the sausage casing, either remove in advance or provide a small bowl to discard the casings.

CURED MEATS are salted and air-dried meats, often pork, such as prosciutto and coppa, and beef bresaola. Other cured meats can include lamb, duck, and wild boar. To serve cured meats, thinly slice and arrange on a board.

PÂTÉ is a blended mix of meats and sweetbreads, such as duck, pork, goose, or chicken livers, with fat, herbs, and spice. The consistency can be slightly chunky (campagne, or country-style) or a smooth and creamy mousse. Serve pâté spread on sliced baguette, toasts, or crostini, and accompany with cornichons (small pickles).

CONFIT is a French term that means "to preserve." Traditionally, it pertains to meats, such as duck, goose, and pork, that are slowly cooked and preserved in their own fat.

RILLETTES are confit meat, poultry, or fish, such as pork, duck, goose, or salmon, that are cooked in their own fat or another fat, such as butter or olive oil, then shredded or chopped. The meat is then packed in fat in small pots or terrines. Serve rillettes spread on sliced baguette or crostini and accompany with cornichons (small pickles). Allow the terrines to stand at room temperature to soften the fat for easy spreading.

CHEESE
HISTORY & TYPES

Cheese is another example of preservation. Cheese-making is an ancient method of preserving easily perishable milk. Thousands of varieties exist, influenced by terroir and milk source (cow, sheep, or goat).

Depending on the origin, climate, milk source, and aging process, cheese types will differ in texture, flavor, and color, which invites endless options for a diverse and visually pleasing cheese board.

TYPES OF CHEESE

FRESH

These young, unripened cheeses have no rind.
They are usually bright white in color, soft,
milky, and mild. Fresh cheeses are delicious
served as a spread; whipped; or embellished with
herbs, spices, ash, or simply a drizzle of olive oil.

EXAMPLES:
Cow: Mozzarella, ricotta
Sheep: Feta
Goat: Feta, fresh goat
    (chèvre frais)

SOFT/BLOOMY RIND

Bloomy rind cheeses are generally mild, sweet, creamy, and buttery. As they age, their flavor becomes more intense with earthy, mushroom notes, and their interior (paste) becomes soft and runny.

EXAMPLES:

Cow: Brie, Camembert, Saint-André, Brillat-Savarin, Mt. Tam Triple Crème, Blue Castello

Sheep: Dirt Lover, Brebirousse d'Argental

Goat: Brie, Humboldt Fog, Truffle Tremor, Cabra

Blend: La Tur, Robiola

SEMIHARD

Semihard cheeses are smooth, buttery, nutty, and earthy with edible rinds. They include younger versions of aged hard cheeses, such as Gouda, Cheddar, or Pecorino.

EXAMPLES:

Cow: Jarlsberg, Emmental, Gruyère, Fontina Valle d'Aosta, Morbier, Comté, Tomme, Double Gloucester

Sheep: Manchego, young Pecorinos, P'tit Basque, Ossau-Iraty

Goat: Garrotxa, Gouda

AGED/HARD

Aged hard cheeses are more concentrated in flavor, with prominent salty, spicy, butterscotch notes. Their texture is hard, often crumbly, and may contain salt crystals.

EXAMPLES:

Cow: Parmigiano-Reggiano, Asiago, Gouda, Cheddar, Gruyère, Mimolette

Sheep: Pecorino Romano, Manchego

Goat: Gouda

WASHED RIND

These soft cheeses are washed with a brine, spirits, wine, or beer. As the cheese ages, it develops a pungent orange-red edible rind, while the interior (paste) may range from mild to earthy and pungent in flavor.

EXAMPLES:

Cow: Époisses de Bourgogne, Reblochon, Saint-Nectaire, Pont l'Évêque, Taleggio, Harbison, Red Hawk

Sheep: Brebirousse d'Argental

Goat: Chevrotin, Drunken Goat (Murcia al Vino)

BLUE-VEINED

Blue veins are formed in these cheeses from a blue mold that grows on their surface and interior. Blue cheeses range from sweet and creamy to sharp and piquant, and their texture can vary from soft to crumbly.

EXAMPLES:

Cow: Gorgonzola, Stilton, Fourme d'Ambert, Danablu, Blue Castello, Point Reyes Original Blue, Maytag Blue
Sheep: Roquefort
Goat: Humboldt Fog
Blend: Cabrales

GIVE ME A GOOD
SHARP KNIFE AND
A GOOD SHARP
CHEESE AND I'M
A HAPPY MAN.

—GEORGE R. R. MARTIN

BOARD
BASICS

A guide to arranging a charcuterie and cheese board.

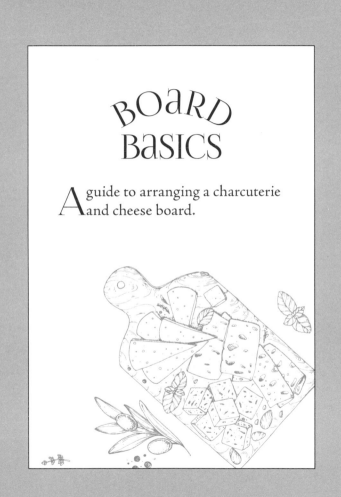

WHAT GROWS TOGETHER
GOES TOGETHER

While it's tempting to arrange a random assortment of meat and cheese on a board, it's helpful to gather ingredients that share a sense of place or terroir, a season or holiday, or a theme. Select cheese and meat that come from the same country or region, or provide a variety of shapes, colors, and garnishes that reflect a season or holiday.

VARIETY

Within your framework, provide an array of shapes, colors, flavors, and textures to appeal to taste and visuals.

INVITE INTERACTION

Make your board interactive. Partially slice salami, then provide a knife to allow slicing. Do not preslice all the cheese, if at all. Cut a few pieces to show how to continue cutting a block, wedge, or round. Provide dips and spreads for self-serving. Arrange nibbles that are easily picked up with fingers or toothpicks, such as sliced fruit, nuts, and olives.

CHOOSE A BOARD

Boards come in different sizes and shapes, such as rectangular, square, oval, or round. Select a sturdy board or surface for arranging the food, and a surface on which you can cut, such as wood, stone, slate. Make sure the surface is food friendly and, if not dishwasher friendly, then hand-washable. The number of servings will dictate the size or number of boards needed.

SUGGESTED SERVING AND BOARD SIZES

+ 3 to 4 ounces combined meat and cheese per person as an appetizer
+ 6 to 8 ounces per person as a main course
+ 2 to 4 guests: Small board with 3 types of cheese, 1 to 2 meats, 0 to 1 dip
+ 6 to 8 guests: Large board with 4 to 5 types of cheese, 2 to 3 meats, 1 to 2 dips
+ 8 or more guests: Extra large or 2 boards, 6 to 7 types of cheese, 3 to 4 meats, 2 dips

TIPS FOR CHOOSING CHEESE

- Include a variety of milk types, including cow, sheep, and goat.
- Offer a range of cheese types, including soft, bloomy, semihard, aged, blue, or washed rind.
- Vary the flavor strengths, from fresh and soft to mild and semihard, to sharp aged, pungent washed rind, and blue.
- Vary the colors and rinds, including white, yellow, and orange paste with bloomy, waxed, washed rinds, or ash, herb, or peppercorn coating.
- Mix up the shapes with blocks, wedges, half-rounds, and whole rounds.
- Vary the textures with soft and creamy, semifirm and hard, and crumbly cheese.
- Choose an odd number of cheeses for the board, especially on small or medium-sized boards.

+ Serve at room temperature. When cheese is refrigerated, the fat in the cheese hardens. Allow the cheese to come to room temperature before serving for the best consistency and full flavor.
+ Provide a separate knife for each cheese. Don't pre-slice all the cheese (if at all) or begin to slice as a guide.

TIPS FOR CHOOSING CHARCUTERIE

+ Choose a variety of charcuterie that complements or matches the provenance of the cheese.
+ Select a variety of textures, such as fatty, hard, dry, chunky pâté, creamy mousse.
+ Select a range of flavor strengths to include mild and sweet, aromatic (herbs, garlic), and spicy.
    + Fan or overlap salami slices. Ruffle or roll soft dried meat slices, such as prosciutto.
        + As an option, partially preslice a salami, then provide a knife to continue slicing.

JARCUTERIE

Put a lid on the traditional cheese and charcuterie board, and stuff it into a jar. Pack your favorite board ingredients into individual serving glasses for a fun and trendy alternative that also ensures safe nibbling. Arrange the jars on a table for easy grabbing, or pack them up for picnics.

To make, simply layer the ingredients in 4- to 6-ounce glasses or mason jars. Start with individual nibbles, such as nuts, dried fruit, and cheese cubes. Use toothpicks to spear olives, cheese wedges, and folded salami or dried meat slices. Insert carrots or celery sticks, bread sticks, or cheese sticks. Garnish with an Easter radish or a few berries, a sprig or two of rosemary and thyme, or an edible flower. These decorative mini-arrangements will be the hit of your next gathering.

CHOOSE FRUIT AND VEGETABLE ACCOMPANIMENTS

Let fruit and vegetables do double duty as finger food and decoration. Choose seasonal fruit and vegetables with an eye for color, such as reds and greens for the winter holiday season or orange and purple for the fall.

Fresh Fruit: Grapes, berries, and sliced fruit, such as apples, pears, figs, persimmons, and stone fruit (Cut the fruit in slices or wedges, or arrange grape bunches and berries for easy finger food)

Dried Fruit: Figs, prunes, apricots, cranberries

Select Seasonal Vegetables as Nibbles and Crudités: Radishes, bell peppers slices, broccolini spears, carrot and celery sticks, cucumber wedges, cherry tomatoes

21

BREADS AND CRISPS

Just like cheese, choose a variety of shapes, textures, and heartiness. Provide gluten-free crackers as a thoughtful option. Arrange a limited amount of bread and crackers on the board without overwhelming or crowding. The breads can be replenished or provided in a separate bowl or basket to the side as a back-up.

+ Baguette
+ Fruit and Nut Loaf Breads
+ Crisp Breads
+ Homemade Crostini *(pg. 113)*
+ Crackers
+ Spiced Pita Chips *(pg. 116)*
+ Gluten-free Crackers

ON THE SIDE AND IN A BOWL

Add dips, spreads, condiments, and nibbles to invite interaction, to complement flavors and themes, and to accessorize the board.

Dips and Spreads: Tapenade, chutney, relish, hummus

Condiments: Honey, mustard, pesto, aioli

Nibbles: Nuts, olives, pickles, chocolate

DECORATION AND BLING

Finish with decorative seasonal food-safe garnishes, such as sprigs of herbs, baby buds, edible flowers, decorative leaves, and twigs.

Add whole seasonal produce, such as crab apples, miniature pumpkins and gourds, baby artichokes, pomegranate wedges, cinnamon sticks, dried orange slices, and pink peppercorn sprigs.

TOOLS & VESSELS

Provide a variety of utensils for cutting and serving, including specialty knives, cocktail forks, small spoons, and toothpicks.

CHARCUTERIE AND CHEESE KNIVES

Provide a separate knife for each cheese:

№1 Soft cheese knife with rounded edge, with holes to prevent sticking for fresh cheese, Brie-style cheese, bloomy

№2 Pronged cheese knife for soft or semihard cheese

№3 Slim-blade knife with minimal surface for soft cheese and pâté

№4 Flat-paddle cheese knife for semisoft or hard aged cheese to cut shards and wedges

№5 Mini cleaver for semihard, hard aged cheese

№6 Sharp-pointed tip for hard cheese

№7 Steak knife for salami

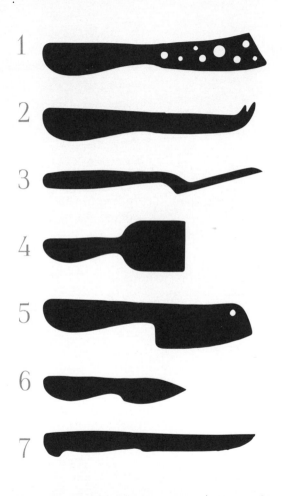

VESSELS

+ Include a variety of small vessels to separate and contain cheese, small crackers, nibbles, and crudités.

+ Place soft or runny cheese on small plates or tiles to capture any oozing cheese.

+ Use a small cheese dome for pungent cheese.

+ Use sturdy leaves and vegetables as vessels to hold nibbles and crudités, such as radicchio, kale, and chicory leaves, or hollowed bell peppers or small cabbages.

ASSEMBLE

- Layer it! Build layers for visual variety, to add height, contain ingredients, and protect surfaces.
- Arrange large, sturdy leaves, such as collard greens, kale, or chard leaves, as a decorative surface on the board.
- Place tiles, small boards, or plates to differentiate and to hold or contain runny or crumbly cheese.
- Arrange and space out the cheese first.
- Place any bowls for dips, spreads, and nibbles.
- Place large grape bunches, if using.
- Arrange the meat: layer, fan, and weave the slices around the cheese, grapes, and bowls.
- Place additional small nibbles, such as sliced fruit, dried fruit, crudités, or nuts.
- Garnish with sprigs, herbs, flowers, or small leaves.

TIPS:

+ Negative space is okay. You don't need to completely cover the board. A little space between items is also decorative.
+ Labeling is optional. It can be helpful to identify cheese sources to address any milk intolerances, such as cow's milk.

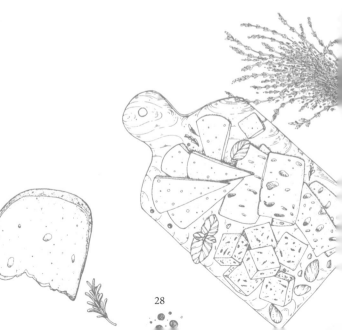

HOST a TASTING PARTY

+ Select a region or theme.
+ Choose 5 to 6 cheeses to taste.
+ Provide either a variety of sources (cow, sheep, goat, blue) or focus on one source (goat cheese, for instance).
+ Taste cheese in a progression from younger to older, milder to stronger.
+ Provide slices of charcuterie that complement the cheese theme.

- Provide simple nibbles to pair with the cheese to cleanse the palate between tastings, such as baguette slices or neutrally flavored crackers, almonds, dried fruit.
- Pair individual wines or beer with each cheese, or two to three options that are compatible with several cheeses.
- Provide notes, paper, and pens for writing.

BOARD INSPIRATION

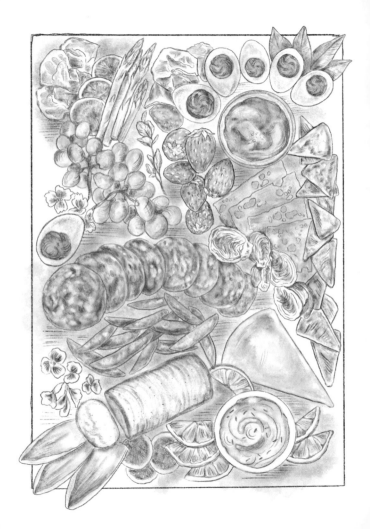

SPRING BLOOM

Spring is the season of new beginnings. Baby leaves, sprigs, and shoots sprout in the garden and arrive at the markets. Accentuate your board with the subtle pastel colors of spring: pale greens, yellow, and white. Lean toward more delicate, fresh cheeses and meat, such as prosciutto. For an Easter board, highlight yellows and white, and feel free to add a few deviled eggs to round out the theme.

CHEESE

Fresh: Goat cheese log with ash

Bloomy Rind: Brie de Meaux, Brillat-Savarin, Humboldt Fog

Semihard: Jarlsberg, Irish Cheddar, P'tit Basque

Hard: Aged Gruyère, Manchego, aged goat Gouda

Washed Rind: Saint-Nectaire, Reblochon, Red Hawk

Blue-Veined: Blue Castello, Gorgonzola

MEAT

Prosciutto, soppressata, fennel salami (finocchiona), duck or chicken liver mousse

DIPS

Sweet Pea Dip *(pg. 80)*, Whipped Ricotta *(pg. 64)*

FRUIT
Strawberries, green grapes

CRUDITÉS
Fennel, blanched asparagus, snap peas,
watermelon radish slices, Easter radishes,
endive leaves

BITES AND BLING
Deviled eggs, lemons, baby artichokes,
edible flowers, mint sprigs

SIPS
Cocktail: Bees' Knees *(pg. 121)*
Wine: Pinot Gris, Pinot Noir, Grenache
Beer: Hoppy, floral, citrus notes; witbier,
    pale ale, light IPAs

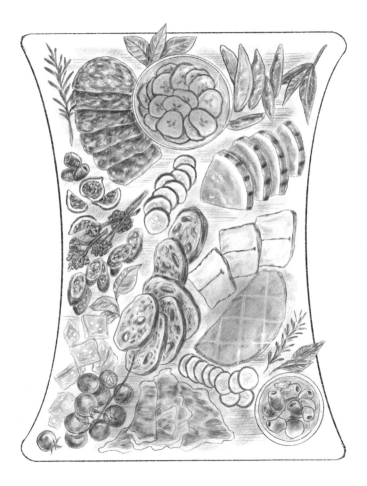

SUMMER SUN

Summer is sunny and vibrant. Let your board reflect its abundance. Show off the season's produce, and be bold in your color choices. Choose salty garnishes to offset the heat, such as olives and tapenade. And if you are celebrating July 4th or Bastille Day, feel free to add a little red, white, and blue (berry) bling.

CHEESE

Fresh: Marinated Feta or Goat Cheese (*pg. 62*)

Bloomy Rind: Mt. Tam Triple Crème, Humboldt Fog, La Tur

Semihard: Comté, Manchego, Morbier

Hard: Aged goat Gouda, Mimolette, Parmigiano-Reggiano

Washed Rind: Brebirousse d'Argental, Taleggio, Harbison

Blue-Veined: Roquefort, Point Reyes Original Blue, Maytag Blue

MEAT

Prosciutto, Genoa salami, garlic salami, chorizo

DIPS

Beet Hummus (*pg. 84*), Green Olive Tapenade (*pg. 102*)

FRUIT
Red and green grapes, strawberries, melon slices, stone fruit slices, fresh figs

CRUDITÉS
Cherry tomatoes, snap peas, bell peppers, cucumbers, watermelon radishes, broccolini

BITES AND BLING
Quick Pickles *(pg. 104)*, edible flowers; parsley, mint, and rosemary sprigs

SIPS
Cocktail: Summer Sangria *(pg. 122)*
Wine: Rosé, Sauvignon Blanc, Grenache
Beer: Light, fruity, citrus notes; lagers, witbier, pale ale, sours

Fall Harvest

The fall season glows in burnished colors of greens, oranges, and reds. Woody garnishes, such as twigs and roots, as well as rustic crisps and crackers complete the rustic picture. Rich cheese and heftier charcuterie are perfect pairings with the cool weather.

CHEESE

Fresh: Herb-coated fresh goat

Bloomy Rind: Camembert, Truffle Tremor, La Tur

Semihard: P'tit Basque, Tomme, Double Gloucester

Hard: Aged Gouda, Beaufort, sharp Cheddar

Washed Rind: Red Hawk, Reblochon, Chevrotin

Blue-Veined: Fourme d'Ambert, Danablu, Point Reyes Original Blue

MEAT

Candied Bacon Chips *(pg. 76)*, coppa, Calabrese peppered salami, country-style pâté

FRUIT

Red grapes, apples, pears, persimmons, fresh figs, dried fruit

DIPS

Apple Chili Relish *(pg. 90)*, Dried Fig and Rosemary Jam *(pg. 87)*, Sweet Potato Hummus *(pg. 84)*

CRUDITÉS

Heirloom carrots, red and orange bell peppers, cauliflower, broccoli

BITES AND BLING

Corn nuts, walnuts, pecans, mini-pumpkins, gourds, kales, rosemary and thyme sprigs, burdock root

SIPS

Cocktail: Maple–Bourbon Old Fashioned *(pg. 125)*

Wine: Chardonnay, Viognier, Pinot Noir, Zinfandel

Beer: Hoppy, dark, spiced; big IPAs, amber ale, porter, hard cider

GERMAN
OKTOBERFEST

Arrange plenty of salami, cooked ham, and mini-sausages; include German cheeses, such as Tilsit, German Emmental, Bavaria Blu, bloomy Cambozola, and washed rind Limburger. Arrange pretzel breads, pumpernickel, and dark rye bread slices. Accompany with mustard, pickles, and sauerkraut. Serve with German beer.

HALLOWEEN

Choose aged and crumbly cheese, blue-veined cheese, and cheese encased in ash. Arrange orange- and white-colored cheese, such as aged Gouda, Mimolette, and Cheddar cheese encased in black wax. Serve chunky, coarse pâtés, rillettes, and pepper-crusted salami. Add creepy garnishes in black and orange colors, such as burdock root, black turnips, gourds, black grapes, and corn nuts. Use spiky purple and dark green kale and chicory leaves for greens.

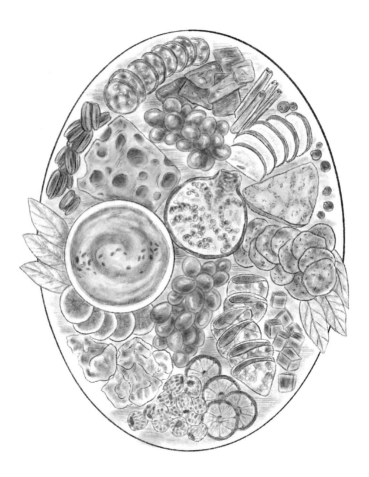

WINTER GLITTER

'Tis the holiday season. Dress up your party boards with a little glam and sparkle. Garnish with festive red, white, and green colors, or lean towards blues and gold for Hannukah. Choose bright, glistening fruit, such as raspberries, pomegranate, and strawberries, and add extra-sweet bling in the form of chocolate and candied nuts.

CHEESE

Fresh: Fresh goat with pink and black peppercorns

Bloomy Rind: Saint-André, Brebirousse d'Argental, La Tur

Semihard: Emmental, P'tit Basque, Tomme

Hard: Aged Gruyère, aged Cheddar, Parmigiano-Reggiano

Washed Rind: Époisses de Bourgogne, Saint-Nectaire, Red Hawk

Blue-Veined: Stilton, Roquefort

MEAT

Prosciutto, peppered salami, wine salami, Duck Rillettes *(pg. 74)*, Smoked Trout Mousse *(pg. 72)*

DIPS

Beet Hummus *(pg. 84)*, Dried Fig and Rosemary Jam *(pg. 87)*

FRUIT
Dried fruit, purple grapes, blackberries, raspberries, pomegranate

CRUDITÉS
Fennel, torpedo and watermelon radishes, carrots, endive spears, radicchio

BITES AND BLING
Chocolate–Chili Almond Bark *(pg. 106)*, pecans, chocolate- or sugar-coated almonds, dried oranges, fresh cranberries, cinnamon sticks, pink peppercorns

SIPS
Cocktail: Champagne Cosmopolitan *(pg. 127)*
Wine: Cabernet Sauvignon, Merlot, Champagne
Beer: Dark, rich, spiced notes; dark lager, pilsner, stout, porter, Christmas brews

ALPINE FONDUE

CHEESE

Bloomy Rind: Vacherin Mont d'Or, Chevrotin

Semihard: Emmental, Raclette, Appenzeller, Tomme de Savoie

Hard: Aged Gruyère, Beaufort

Washed Rind: Reblochon, Vacherin Fribourgeois

MEAT

Viande des Grisons or bresaola, prosciutto, capicola or coppa, cooked sausages (sliced, served warm)

DIPS
Baked Vacherin (*pg. 66*)

FRUIT
Apples, pears, grapes

VEGETABLES
Boiled baby potatoes

BITES AND BLING
Cornichons, pickled onions, mustard

SIPS
Wine: Riesling, Sancerre, Gamay

FRENCH APÉRITIF

CHEESE

Fresh: Marinated Goat Cheese *(pg. 62)*

Bloomy Rind: Brie de Meaux, Camembert, Bûche de Chèvre, Saint-Marcellin

Semihard: Ossau-Iraty, Comté, Morbier, Tomme

Hard: Mimolette, Beaufort

Washed Rind: Reblochon, Saint-Nectaire, Pont l'Évêque, Époisses de Bourgogne

Blue-Veined: Roquefort, Fourme d'Ambert

MEAT

Sauçisson sec, garlic sausage, pâté de campagne, Duck Rillettes (*pg. 74*)

DIPS

Green Olive Tapenade (*pg. 102*), Sweet Pea Dip (*pg. 80*)

FRUIT

Grapes, apricots, apples, pears

CRUDITÉS

Radishes, blanched asparagus, green beans, cherry tomatoes

BITES AND BLING

Walnuts, cornichons, lavender honey, Marinated Olives (*pg. 99*)

SIPS

Wine: Chablis, Rosé, Syrah, Burgundy, Mourvèdre

Beer: French pale lager, such as Kronenbourg 1664; hard cider

Italian Antipasti

CHEESE
Fresh: Burrata
Bloomy Soft Rind: Robiola
Semihard: Pecorino Toscano, Pecorino Sardo, Fontina Valle d'Aosta
Hard/Aged: Parmigiano-Reggiano, Grana Padano, Asiago
Washed Rind: Taleggio, Toma Piemontese
Blue-Veined: Gorgonzola

MEAT
Prosciutto, coppa, 'nduja, soppressata, fennel salami

DIPS

Whipped Ricotta *(pg. 64)*; trio of bowls with extra-virgin olive oil, balsamic vinegar, sea salt

FRUIT

Melon, blood oranges, oranges, figs

CRUDITÉS

Fennel, radicchio, sweet peppers, cherry tomatoes

BITES AND BLING

Olives; Prosciutto Rolls with Arugula, Fennel, and Mint *(pg. 69)*; Parmesan Crisps *(pg. 110)*; Homemade Crostini *(pg. 113)*

SIPS

Wine: Pinot Grigio, Vermentino, Nebbiolo, Sangiovese
Beer: Italian fruity lager, such as Peroni

Spanish Tapas

CHEESE
Bloomy Rind: Cabra
Semihard: Garrotxa, Mahón
Hard: Manchego
Washed Rind: Drunken Goat (Murcia al Vino)
Blue-Veined: Cabrales

MEAT
Jamón Serrano, Jamón Ibérico, chorizo

DIP
Red Pepper Romesco Sauce (*pg. 82*)

BITES AND BLING

Marcona almonds, quince paste, roasted Padrón (shishito) peppers, Homemade Crostini *(pg. 113)*

SIPS

Cocktail: Summer Sangria *(pg. 122)*
Wine: Cava, Albariño, Tempranillo, Malbec, sherry
Beer: Spanish lager, such as Estrella Galicia

INVEST YOURSELF, YOUR
MONEY, AND YOUR
TIME IN CHEESE.

—Anthony Bourdain, *Medium Raw:
A Bloody Valentine to the World of
Food and the People Who Cook*

RECIPES
&
BASICS

GOOD CHEESE
WANTS GOOD
COMPANIONS.

—JAMES BEARD

D·I·Y
MEAT & CHEESE

RECIPES

MARINATED FETA
OR GOAT CHEESE

This is a recipe template for marinating a variety of fresh cheese, including feta, goat cheese, and mozzarella. A lemon- and garlic-infused olive oil enriches the mild flavor of fresh cheese while it marinates. To infuse the oil, it must be warmed first, so be sure to cool it completely before pouring over the cheese to prevent the cheese from melting.

OIL

⅔ cup extra-virgin olive oil

3 strips lemon peel, from a vegetable peeler

2 sprigs fresh thyme

1 sprig fresh rosemary

1 clove garlic, peeled and thinly sliced

½ teaspoon black peppercorns

¼ teaspoon crushed red pepper flakes

8 ounces feta cheese, drained, cut in ¾-inch cubes (or one 6 to 8-ounce goat cheese log, cut in ½-inch-thick slices)

Spiced Pita Chips (*pg. 116*) or Homemade Crostini (*pg. 113*), for serving

1   Combine the oil ingredients in a small saucepan over medium-low heat. Heat the oil until very warm, without coming to a boil, to infuse the flavors.

2   Remove from the heat and cool to room temperature.

3   Place the cheese in a shallow bowl or glass container. Pour the oil over the cheese and gently stir to combine.

4   Cover and refrigerate for 3 hours or overnight, stirring once or twice. Serve at room temperature with crostini or pita toasts.

WHIPPED RICOTTA

Whipping ricotta transforms this cheese into a light and fluffy dip. Simple aromatics will infuse it, such as lemon for a savory option or a drizzle of honey for a sweeter touch. Be sure to use whole milk ricotta for best results.

1 cup whole milk ricotta

2 tablespoons extra-virgin olive oil

2 teaspoons fresh lemon juice

¼ teaspoon kosher salt

⅛ teaspoon black pepper

Freshly grated lemon zest, optional

Honey, optional

1   Combine the ricotta, olive oil, lemon juice, salt, and black pepper in a food processor. Process until light and smooth, and taste for seasoning.

2   Add a generous pinch of fresh lemon zest or a little honey, if desired.

3   Transfer to a small bowl with a lid and refrigerate until use or up to 2 days.

4   Serve as a dip for crudités and bread.

Baked
Vacherin

MAKES 6 TO 8 SERVINGS

This is a traditional method to serve Vacherin Mont d'Or, which is packaged in a light wooden box. If it's difficult to source, Camembert cheese (also packaged in a wooden box) can be substituted for the Vacherin. Depending on the thickness of the cheese, the cooking times may vary.

1 round box (about 1 pound) Vacherin Mont d'Or cheese, room temperature

1 clove garlic, peeled and cut into slivers

2 tablespoons dry white wine, such as Sauvignon Blanc

Freshly ground black pepper

Baguette slices

Cornichons

Pickled onions

Boiled baby potatoes

1 Heat the oven to 400°F.

2 Remove the lid of the cheese box. Tightly wrap the cheese box with foil, leaving the top exposed. Place on a rimmed baking sheet.

3 Make 6 to 8 incisions in the top rind of the cheese. Insert the slivers of garlic in the incisions. Drizzle the wine over the cheese.

4 Bake in the oven until the cheese is melty, about 20 minutes.

5 Remove from the oven and garnish with freshly ground black pepper. Serve warm with baguette slices and cornichons, pickled onions, and baby potatoes for dipping.

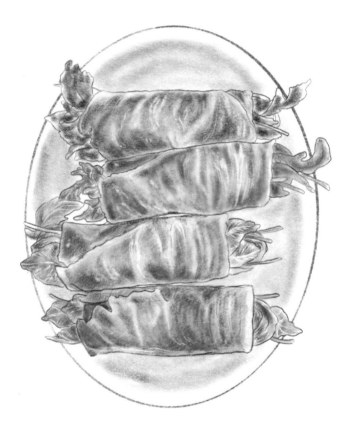

PROSCIUTTO ROLLS
WITH ARUGULA, FENNEL, and MINT

These rolls are fresh and bright. Soft, supple prosciutto envelops crisp fennel shards, leafy mint, and nutty parmesan shavings for a wonderful blend of textures, flavor, and salt. The rolls take a little time to assemble, but the good news is that they can be prepared in advance and refrigerated for up to 4 hours before serving. For smaller rolls, halve the prosciutto slices lengthwise to make 16 strips, each about 1 inch wide.

recipe continues on the next page

8 slices prosciutto

Extra-virgin olive oil

Freshly ground black pepper

Zest from 1 lemon

2 cups packed arugula leaves

2 medium fennel bulbs

**4 ounces (about ½ cup) Parmesan cheese,
shaved with a vegetable peeler**

16 medium-large mint leaves

1 Place one strip of prosciutto on a work surface, with a short end closest to you. Lightly brush with olive oil.

2 Sprinkle with black pepper and a pinch of lemon zest. Lay 4 to 6 arugula leaves horizontally at the base.

3   Remove the cores and fronds from the fennel. Halve the bulbs lengthwise, then thinly slice each half lengthwise.

4   Place a few shards of fennel and Parmesan over the arugula. Top with a mint leaf.

5   Roll up from the base, wrapping the prosciutto tightly around the vegetables, and continue to roll, placing 1 or 2 additional arugula leaves in the fold as you roll up. Place the roll seam side down on a platter. Repeat with remaining ingredients. The rolls may be prepared up to 4 hours in advance of serving.

6   Cover with plastic wrap and refrigerate. Let them stand at room temperature for 20 to 30 minutes before serving. Before serving, lightly spritz with olive oil or lemon juice, if desired.

SMOKED TROUT MOUSSE

The combination of a rich and creamy smoked fish mousse and crunchy toasted almonds is elegant and addictive. The mousse can be prepared and refrigerated for up to 2 days in advance of serving, which is ideal for entertaining. Smoked mackerel or warm smoked salmon can be substituted for the trout.

MOUSSE

8 ounces smoked trout, skin and pinbones removed

6 ounces cream cheese, room temperature

¼ cup grated yellow onion, with juices

¼ cup fresh lemon juice

1 teaspoon Worcestershire sauce

1 teaspoon black pepper, plus extra for garnish

½ teaspoon Tabasco

Thinly sliced European–style pumpernickel squares or rounds, or baguette slices

⅓ cup almonds, toasted and coarsely chopped

Chopped chives

1 Process the mousse ingredients in a food processor until light and smooth. If too thick, add a little more lemon juice. Taste, and add more Tabasco if desired.

2 Transfer to a small bowl and chill until serving.

3 To serve, smear on pumpernickel bread or baguette slices. Top with the almonds and chives.

DUCK
RILLETTES

Duck rillettes are a time-intensive preparation that yields rich results. An easy shortcut is to purchase prepared duck confit legs and duck fat, which will significantly reduce the prep time for this unctuous delicacy. Let the rillettes stand at room temperature for 30 minutes before serving to allow the fat to soften.

4 prepared duck legs confit

¼ cup duck fat, melted, plus more as needed

1 tablespoon Calvados (apple brandy), optional

½ teaspoon coarsely ground black peppercorns

Kosher salt

1   Discard the skin from the duck legs. Place the meat in a medium bowl and shred with two forks.

2   Add the Calvados, if using, then add the duck fat, 1 tablespoon at a time, to moisten and soften. If the mixture is too thick, add additional fat or high-quality chicken or duck stock.

3   Season with the black peppercorns and salt to taste (the mixture will be salty).

4   Pack into individual ramekins or mason jars. If desired, spread a thin layer of fat over the top of the ramekins.

5   Cover with foil and refrigerate for at least 24 hours or up to 1 week.

CANDIED
BACON CHIPS

MAKES ABOUT 24 CHIPS

Nothing beats pan-fried bacon; that is, unless you add a little sugar and spice to the mix and bake the bacon until crisp. These sweet and salty bacon chips will leave you wondering whether you should call them a snack or dessert. Either way, they add a unique twist to a selection of charcuterie. Let the bacon chips thoroughly cool once removed from the oven. They will continue to crisp while they cool.

1 cup packed light brown sugar

12 ounces thinly sliced bacon, cut in 2-inch strips

Ground cinnamon and cayenne pepper, for sprinkling

1 Heat the oven to 350°F.

2 Pour the sugar onto a small plate. Dredge the bacon in the sugar to apply a thick coating.

3 Arrange the bacon in a single layer on a rimmed baking sheet lined with parchment paper. Sprinkle the cinnamon and cayenne over the bacon.

4 Bake in the oven until the bacon is golden brown, turning once with a spatula halfway through, about 15 minutes.

5 Remove from the oven and transfer the bacon to a plate lined with parchment paper. Cool completely. The bacon will continue to crisp while it cools.

6 Serve or store in an airtight container in the refrigerator for up to 2 days. Gently reheat in an oven at 300°F for 6 to 8 minutes.

GOOD BREAD AND CORNICHONS, OF COURSE. OTHER PICKLED VEGETABLES ARE GOOD, TOO. AND WINE! IT IS IMPORTANT TO HAVE A BALANCE WITH THE RICH FLAVORS OF PÂTÉ. ALWAYS HAVE WINE WITH PÂTÉ.

—Chef Antoine Westermann of Parisian bistro Le Coq Rico, speaking to *Food Republic* Senior Editor Jess Kapadia

IN a BOWL

DIPS • SPREADS • RELISHES

Sweet Pea Dip | 80

Red Pepper Romesco Sauce | 82

Beet or Sweet Potato Hummus | 84

Dried Fig and Rosemary Jam | 87

Apple Chili Relish | 90

Dried Fruit Chutney | 92

SWEET PEA DIP

This bright dip is best prepared with frozen peas, which maintain their vibrant color and purée beautifully. Because the peas are frozen, this dip can be enjoyed year-round. There's no need to preheat the peas; simply defrost them in the refrigerator or run under warm water to quickly defrost, and drain before using.

1 (16-ounce) package frozen
sweet peas, defrosted

3 tablespoons fresh lemon juice

2 large cloves garlic

2 tablespoons packed finely grated
Pecorino Romano cheese

2 tablespoons extra-virgin olive oil

1 teaspoon kosher salt

½ teaspoon freshly grated lemon zest

½ teaspoon black pepper

¼ teaspoon crushed red pepper flakes

1 Combine all the ingredients in a food processor. Process until smooth. Taste for seasoning.

2 Store in the refrigerate for up to 2 days.

3 Serve with crudités for dipping.

RED PEPPER
ROMESCO SAUCE

MAKES ABOUT 1 CUP

Jarred roasted red peppers lend smoky sweetness to this Spanish-inspired condiment. It's delicious as a dip or spread on crostini. Chile peppers can vary in heat, so taste a small piece when chopping and adjust the amount accordingly to your taste.

2 large roasted red peppers from a jar, drained and coarsely chopped

1 red jalapeño or Fresno pepper, seeds removed and coarsely chopped

¼ cup almonds, toasted

2 cloves garlic, chopped

2 tablespoons tomato paste

1 tablespoon extra-virgin olive oil

1 tablespoon sherry vinegar

1 teaspoon smoked paprika

½ teaspoon ground cumin

½ teaspoon kosher salt

½ teaspoon black pepper

1 Combine all the ingredients in a food processor, and process to blend. Taste for seasoning.

2 Serve immediately or refrigerate for up to 3 days.

BEET OR SWEET POTATO HUMMUS

This hummus gets a sweet and earthy boost from roasted beets or sweet potatoes. They also paint the hummus a stunning color, which makes this dip an eye-popping centerpiece. If using sweet potatoes, peel them first, then cut into large chunks and roast until tender.

1 pound red beets or sweet potatoes, roasted until tender, then skins removed

1 (15-ounce) can chickpeas, drained and rinsed

2 cloves garlic

¼ cup fresh lime juice

¼ cup tahini

1 tablespoon extra-virgin olive oil

2 teaspoons sriracha

1 teaspoon kosher salt

1 teaspoon ground cumin

1 teaspoon ground coriander

½ teaspoon black pepper

Chopped fresh mint or cilantro
leaves, for garnish

1 Place the hummus ingredients in a food processor, and process until smooth. If too thick, add warm water or more olive oil, 1 tablespoon at a time, to achieve your desired consistency. Taste for seasoning.

2 Transfer to a bowl and refrigerate for up to 3 days.

3 Garnish with a drizzle of olive oil and chopped fresh mint or cilantro. Serve with Spiced Pita Chips (*pg. 110*) and crudités.

DRIED FIG and ROSEMARY JAM

MAKES ABOUT 2 CUPS

Dried Mission figs are the best figs to use in this intensely flavored jam. The jam's flavor will develop with time, so try to make it at least 1 day in advance of serving. Use as a spread or as an accompaniment to earthy, pungent cheeses and smoked meats.

recipe continues on the next page

3 cups dried Mission figs (about 12 ounces), stems removed and coarsely chopped

½ cup port wine

½ cup fresh orange juice

¼ cup balsamic vinegar

1 teaspoon freshly grated orange zest

1 sprig fresh rosemary

¼ teaspoon black pepper

Pinch of kosher salt

1 Combine the ingredients in a large saucepan and bring to a simmer over medium heat.

2 Reduce the heat to medium-low, partially cover the pot with a lid, and cook until the figs are soft and the mixture thickens, about 20 minutes, stirring occasionally.

3 Remove from the heat and cool completely. Discard the rosemary sprig. Store in a glass jar for up to 1 week.

MY LAST SUPPER
WOULD BE A
CHARCUTERIE
SMORGASBORD WITH
EVERY KIND OF
MEAT, AND SAUCES
TO DIP THEM IN.

—KELIS

Apple Chill Relish

Inspired by piccalilli, this vibrant relish is a sweet and sharp accompaniment to buttery and piquant cheese. The peppers may vary in heat, so taste a little of each to judge the amount in the relish and adjust to your taste.

1 tablespoon extra-virgin olive oil

1 small yellow onion, chopped

2 medium sweet red peppers, such as bell or pimento, seeded and thinly sliced

1 hot red pepper, such as jalapeño or Fresno, thinly sliced

2 large Granny Smith apples, peeled, cored, and diced

1 cup apple cider vinegar

½ cup golden raisins

⅓ cup packed light brown sugar

**1 tablespoon grated peeled
fresh ginger, with juices**

1 teaspoon yellow mustard seeds

½ teaspoon turmeric

½ teaspoon black pepper

½ teaspoon kosher salt

1 Heat the oil in a large saucepan. Add the onion and sauté until slightly soft, about 2 minutes.

2 Add the peppers and sauté for about 30 seconds more.

3 Add the remaining ingredients. Bring to a simmer and cook over medium heat until the sugar dissolves and the relish thickens, 15 to 20 minutes, stirring frequently.

4 Remove from the heat and cool completely.

5 Transfer to a glass jar and refrigerate for up to 1 week.

DRIED FRUIT CHUTNEY

MAKES ABOUT 2 CUPS

This chutney willingly absorbs a generous assortment of dried fruit and spice—and promises to fill your kitchen with the fragrance of Christmas while it's simmering. Serve it as an accompaniment with sharp and bloomy cheeses and cured meats.

1 small yellow onion, chopped

1 cup chopped dried apricots

1 cup chopped dried prunes

½ cup dried cranberries

½ cup packed light brown sugar

½ cup apple cider vinegar

¼ cup bourbon or dark rum

¼ cup fresh orange juice

1 teaspoon freshly grated orange zest

½ teaspoon ground cinnamon

½ teaspoon ground coriander

¼ teaspoon ground cloves

¼ teaspoon kosher salt

¼ teaspoon black pepper

1 Combine all the ingredients in a medium saucepan over medium heat.

2 Bring to a boil and reduce heat to medium-low. Simmer, uncovered, until the liquid is nearly evaporated and the mixture thickens, about 25 minutes, stirring frequently.

3 Taste for seasoning. Cool to room temperature. Store in the refrigerator for up to 1 week.

WINE AND CHEESE ARE
AGELESS COMPANIONS,
LIKE ASPIRIN AND ACHES,
OR JUNE AND MOON,
OR GOOD PEOPLE AND
NOBLE VENTURES.

—M. F. K. Fisher

NIBBLES

SPICED ALMONDS

MAKES 2 CUPS

The spices and sugar in this recipe elevate the humble almond to a festive cocktail nibble. Pecans and walnuts can be substituted for the almonds in this versatile recipe.

1½ cups raw almonds

2 tablespoons extra-virgin olive oil

1 tablespoon minced fresh rosemary

2 teaspoons kosher salt, plus
more for sprinkling

2 teaspoons sweet paprika

1 teaspoon freshly grated lemon zest

½ teaspoon black pepper

½ teaspoon granulated sugar

¼ teaspoon cayenne pepper

1   Heat the oven to 350°F.

2   Place the almonds in a medium bowl. Add the remaining ingredients and stir to coat.

3   Spread on a rimmed baking sheet lined with parchment paper.

4   Roast in the oven until golden brown and fragrant, about 15 minutes, shaking the pan once or twice.

5   Remove from the oven and sprinkle with additional salt to taste.

6   Store the almonds in an airtight container for up to one week.

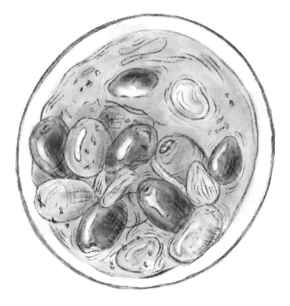

MARINATED OLIVES

MAKES 2 CUPS

These olives are a year-round treat. They are best made ahead of serving to allow the flavors to develop, which is ideal for entertaining. Keep the olives refrigerated and allow them to come to room temperature before serving to bring out their flavor.

recipe continues on the next page

½ cup extra-virgin olive oil

3 cloves garlic,
crushed but intact

2 sprigs fresh thyme

1 bay leaf

Juice and peel from ½ lemon

½ teaspoon black peppercorns

¼ teaspoon crushed
red pepper flakes

2 cups mixed black
and green olives

1   Place the oil, garlic, thyme, bay leaf, lemon juice and zest, peppercorns, and red pepper flakes in a small saucepan.

2   Heat over medium-low heat until warm, but not boiling. Remove from the heat and add the olives.

3   Stir to coat, then let stand until room temperature. Serve or transfer to a glass jar and refrigerate for up to 4 days.

Note: Make sure the garlic cloves are completely submerged in the oil when storing.

GREEN OLIVE TAPENADE

*This tapenade is salty, briny, and fruity.
It's a perfect bite in the warm weather. Try not
to overprocess the tapenade. The consistency
should be finely chopped and not too mushy.*

**2 cups pitted green olives,
such as Castelvetrano or a
mixture of green olives**

**¼ cup raw almonds, toasted
and coarsely chopped**

1 anchovy

1 large clove garlic

2 tablespoons extra-virgin olive oil

1 teaspoon freshly grated lemon zest

½ teaspoon black pepper

1   Place the ingredients in a food processor
    and process to finely chop.

2   Serve at room temperature or refrigerate for
    up to 3 days.

QUICK PICKLES

MAKES 2 POUNDS

Use your favorite summer vegetables for this easy recipe. Include a variety of colors and shapes for fun visuals, both in the jar and on the board. Because the pickling method is quick, use the pickles within 5 days of preparing. If using Kirby cucumbers, pre-salt the cucumbers for 30 minutes, then wipe off moisture before adding.

BRINE

3 cups water

3 cups apple cider vinegar

¼ cup granulated sugar

6 cloves garlic, smashed but intact

3 tablespoons kosher salt

2 bay leaves

2 teaspoons black peppercorns

1 teaspoon fennel seeds

1 teaspoon coriander seeds

1 teaspoon brown mustard seeds

**2 pounds assorted vegetables,
such as cauliflower florets, sliced bell
peppers, baby carrots, green beans,
fennel, sliced Kirby cucumbers**

1 Wash and trim the vegetables as needed.
Tightly pack the vegetables into clear
heatproof jars.

2 Combine the brine ingredients in a large
saucepan. Bring to a boil, stirring to
dissolve the sugar and salt. Pour the brine
over the vegetables.

3 Cover and cool to room temperature.

4 Refrigerate at least 24 hours or up to 5
days. The flavors will develop with time.

CHOCOLATE-CHILI ALMOND BARK

MAKES ABOUT 1 POUND

Chocolate is a great addition to a charcuterie and cheese board, especially during the holiday season. The spices in this bark are optional but recommended. They impart a surprising and pleasant hint of spice and kick of heat without overwhelming the chocolate. Be sure to include the salt as a finishing touch.

12 ounces dark chocolate (70%), coarsely chopped

½ teaspoon ground cinnamon (optional)

½ teaspoon ancho chili powder (optional)

1 cup raw almonds, toasted and coarsely chopped

¾ cup golden raisins

Sea salt

1 Line a baking sheet with parchment paper.

2 Melt two-thirds (or 8 ounces) of the chocolate in the bowl of a double boiler, stirring until smooth. (Alternatively, fill a medium pot with 1 inch of water and bring the water to a bare simmer. Place the chocolate in a heat-resistant bowl, and place the bowl over the pot without touching the water. Stir the chocolate until smooth.)

3 Remove the bowl from the heat and add the remaining chocolate, stirring until smooth. Stir in the cinnamon and chili powder, if using, then add half of the almonds and half of the raisins.

4 Pour the chocolate onto the baking sheet and smooth it out in a thin, even layer with a spatula.

recipe continues on the next page

5 Sprinkle the remaining nuts and raisins over the chocolate, gently pressing them in. Sprinkle with the sea salt.

6 Refrigerate until firm, about 30 minutes. Break into large shards.

7 Refrigerate in an airtight container for up to 1 week.

BEYOND BREAD

Parmesan Crisps | 110

Homemade Crostini | 113

Spiced Pita Chips | 116

PARMESAN CRISPS

*This recipe is extremely simple, and the results
are unmistakably cheesy and salty. In fact,
you might want to double the recipe because
they are so tasty and will disappear quickly.*

1 cup grated Parmesan cheese

**¼ teaspoon coarsely ground
black pepper (optional)**

1 Heat the oven to 400°F.

2 Line a rimmed baking sheet with
parchment paper. Drop 2 tablespoons of
cheese in a mound on the parchment paper.
Press with a spoon to flatten in a circle,
about 2 inches in diameter. Repeat with
the remaining cheese.

3 Sprinkle the black pepper over the mounds, if using.

4 Bake in the oven until golden and crisp, 6 to 8 minutes.

5 Cool completely on the baking sheet. Store in an airtight container at room temperature for up to 2 days.

HOMEMADE CROSTINI

MAKES ABOUT 24 CROSTINI

Crostini are a must-have on a charcuterie and cheese board. They are perfect for smearing with dips, spreads, cheese, and pâté. They are also simple to make and a useful way to use up day-old bread. Once made, the crostini will keep in an airtight container for up to 2 days.

recipe continues on the next page

1 French–style baguette

Extra-virgin olive oil, for brushing

Sea salt, for sprinkling

1 Heat the oven to 400°F. Line a rimmed baking sheet with parchment paper.

2 Slice the baguette on the diagonal ¼- to ½-inch thick. Lightly brush the slices on both sides with olive oil.

3 Arrange in one layer on the baking sheet and lightly season with salt. Bake in the oven until light golden and crisp, about 8 minutes.

4 Turn off the oven and crack the oven door. Let the crostini cool completely in the oven, about 15 minutes. They will continue to crisp as they cool.

5 Store in an airtight container for up to 2 days.

CHEESE, WINE,
AND A FRIEND
MUST BE OLD TO
BE GOOD.

—REINHOLD NIEBUHR

SPICED
PITA CHIPS
MAKES 24 CHIPS

Why buy store-bought pita chips when you can easily make your own? This recipe is another great way to use up days-old bread. The spices are adaptable to your taste. Just be sure to include the salt.

¼ cup extra-virgin olive oil

**½ teaspoon kosher salt,
plus more for sprinkling**

¼ teaspoon garlic powder

¼ teaspoon sweet paprika

¼ teaspoon black pepper

3 large pita breads

1 Heat the oven to 350°F.

2 Whisk the oil, salt, garlic powder, sweet paprika, and black pepper in a small bowl. Brush the pita on both sides with the oil mixture.

3 Cut the pita into 8 to 12 wedges. Spread in 1 layer on a rimmed baking sheet lined with parchment paper and season the pitas with additional salt.

4 Transfer to the oven and bake until golden brown, about 15 minutes.

5 Turn off the oven and crack the door. Let the pita cool in the oven until crisp, about 15 minutes.

6 Store in an airtight container for up to 2 days.

. . . GOOD COMPANY,
GOOD WINE, GOOD
WELCOME, CAN MAKE
GOOD PEOPLE.

—William Shakespeare, *Henry VIII*

COCKTAILS

Bees' Knees | 121

Summer Sangria | 122

Maple–Bourbon Old Fashioned | 125

Champagne Cosmopolitan | 127

Bees' Knees

MAKES 1

Greet spring with this fresh, citrusy
cocktail sweetened with honey syrup.

2 ounces gin

¾ ounce fresh lemon juice

½ ounce honey syrup

Lemon twist, for garnish

1 To make honey syrup, whisk 2 parts warm water to 1 part runny honey until combined.

2 Add the gin, lemon juice, and honey syrup to a shaker with ice, and shake until well chilled.

3 Strain into a chilled cocktail glass. Garnish with a lemon twist.

SUMMER SANGRIA

A summer party is not complete without sangria. A fruity red wine and the chopped fruit will impart sweetness to the sangria while it chills. The additional sugar is optional and to your taste.

1 (750-mL) bottle fruity red wine, such as Syrah or Grenache

½ cup fresh orange juice

⅓ cup orange-flavored liqueur, such as Cointreau

1 to 2 tablespoons light brown sugar or maple syrup (optional)

1 navel orange, halved and thinly sliced

1 lemon, halved, seeded, and thinly sliced

1 Granny Smith apple, cored and diced

1 Combine the wine, orange juice, and orange liqueur in a pitcher.

2 Add the sugar, if using, and stir to dissolve. Stir in the fruit.

3 Refrigerate for at least 3 hours or up to 6 hours. Serve with ice.

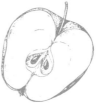

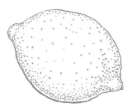

Maple-Bourbon Old Fashioned

MAKES 1

Bourbon is on the menu in the fall, and this recipe amplifies the season with the addition of maple syrup.

recipe continues on the next page

2 ounces bourbon whiskey

1 teaspoon maple syrup

4 dashes Angostura bitters

Ice, for serving

Orange peel, for garnish

Cocktail cherry, for garnish

1 In a lowball glass, stir the bourbon, maple syrup, and bitters. Add a large ice cube.

2 Use a knife to remove a 1-inch strip of the orange peel. Squeeze the orange peel into the drink to release the oils.

3 Gently run the peel around the edge of the glass, then place the peel in the glass. Garnish with a cherry, if using. Serve immediately.

CHAMPAGNE COSMOPOLITAN

MAKES 1

This glittery cocktail is a party-worthy addition to any celebration. It can easily be multiplied for any number of people.

1½ ounces vodka

½ ounce orange-flavored liqueur, such as Cointreau or Gran Marnier

½ ounce cranberry juice

½ ounce fresh lime juice

Dash of prepared simple syrup

Brut Champagne

recipe continues on the next page

1 To make simple syrup, heat equal parts water and granulated sugar, stirring to dissolve the sugar. Cool to room temperature.

2 Add the vodka, orange-flavored liqueur, cranberry juice, lime juice, and simple syrup to a shaker with ice, and shake until well chilled.

3 Strain into a martini glass and top with Champagne.